CW00429615

THIS BOOK BELONGS TO:

Shop our other books at
www.sillyslothpress.com

For questions and customer service, email us at
support@sillyslothpress.com

© Silly Sloth Press. All rights reserved. No part of this publication may
be reproduced, distributed, or transmitted, in any form or by any means,
including photocopying, recording, or other electronic or mechanical
methods, without prior written permission of the publisher, except in the
case of brief quotations embodied in critical reviews and certain other
noncommercial uses permitted by copyright law.

JOKE 1

Q: WHAT DO A DENTIST AND A PROCTOLOGIST HAVE IN COMMON?

A: THEY BOTH TELL YOU TO OPEN UP AND YOU GO AHH.

JOKE 2

Q: WHY DID THE OLD LADY COVER HER MOUTH WITH HER HANDS WHEN SHE SNEEZED?

A: TO CATCH HER FALSE TEETH.

JOKE 3

Q: WHAT DO YOU CALL SOMEONE WHO DISCRIMINATES AGAINST PEOPLE WHO WEAR BRACES?

A: A BRACIST.

JOKE 4

Q: WHO GAVE BIG FOOT MONEY FOR HIS BABY TEETH?

A: THE TOOTH HAIRY.

JOKE 5

Q: WHY DO SOCIAL JUSTICE WARRIES DESPISE DENTISTS?

A: BECAUSE THEY MAKE TEETH STRAIGHT AND WHITE.

JOKE 6

Q: WHY DO VAMPIRES BRUSH AND FLOSS DAILY?

A: TO AVOID BAT BREATH.

JOKE 7

Q: WHAT DETECTIVE FINDS MISSING TEETH?

A: A TOOTH SLEUTH.

JOKE 8

PATIENT: HOW MUCH TO HAVE THIS TOOTH PULLED?

DENTIST: $300

PATIENT: $300 FOR JUST A FEW MINUTES WORK?

DENTIST: I CAN EXTRACT IT VERY SLOWLY IF YOU LIKE.

JOKE 9

Q: WHAT DOES AN ORTHODONTIST DO ON A THRILL RIDE?

A: SHE BRACES HERSELF.

JOKE 10

Q: WHY ARE TEETH SO TRUSTWORTHY?

A: THEY LEARN FROM THE TRUTH FAIRY.

JOKE 11

Q: WHY COULDN'T THE FAMILY LOCATE THE DENTIST'S GRAVE?

A: THERE WAS NO PLAQUE ON IT.

JOKE 12

Q: WHAT DO YOU CALL AN ORAL HYGIENE PRODUCT FOR THE BRAIN?

A: NEURAL CREST.

JOKE 13

Q: WHY DID THE MIDDLE SCHOOL TEETH GET IN TROUBLE AT THE SCHOOL DANCE?

A: THEY WERE GRINDING.

JOKE 14

Q: WHY DID THE JEWEL THIEF ROB THE DENTIST OFFICE?

A: HE HEARD THEY HAD PEARLY WHITES.

JOKE 15

Q: WHICH COUNTRY'S CITIZENS HAVE THE PRETTIEST TEETH?

A: BRUSSIA.

JOKE 16

FAN: I'VE ALWAYS ADMIRED YOU. ARE YOUR TEETH YOUR OWN?

ACTOR: WHOSE DO YOU THINK THEY ARE?

JOKE 17

Q: WHAT KIND OF CONCERTS DO KIDS WITH BRACES GO TO?

A: HEAVY METAL.

JOKE 18

Q: WHO BRINGS TEETH PRESENTS ON CHRISTMAS EVE?

A: SANTA FLOSS.

JOKE 19

Q: WHO SHOWS TEETH HOW TO CHEW?

A: SCHOOL TEETHERS.

JOKE 20

Q: WHAT DO YOU CALL A BOOMERANG MADE OF TEETH?

A: I DON'T REMEMBER THE PUNCHLINE AND IT WILL PROBABLY COME BACK TO BITE ME.

JOKE 21

Q: WHY COULDN'T THE DENTIST HELP THE GIRL WHO ATE GLUE?

A: HER LIPS WERE SEALED.

JOKE 22

Q: WHAT'S THE DIFFERENCE BETWEEN A DENTIST AND A SADIST?

A: A DENTIST HAS NEWER MAGAZINES.

JOKE 23

Q: WHAT HAPPENS WHEN YOU DON'T BRUSH YOUR TEETH FOR TEN YEARS?

A: TOOTH DECADE.

JOKE 24

Q: WHAT WAS THE TOOTH'S BOOK REPORT ON?

A: ENAMEL FARM.

JOKE 25

Q: HOW CAN YOU CUT PAPER USING ONLY YOUR MOUTH?

A: USE YOUR INCISORS.

JOKE 26

FATHER: I HAVE AN AWFUL TOOTHACHE.

SON: I'D HAVE IT TAKEN OUT IF IT WAS MINE.

FATHER: YES, IF IT WAS YOURS, I WOULD, TOO.

JOKE 27

Q: WHAT DO YOU CALL BAD BREATH THAT SNEAKS UP ON YOU?

A: NINJAVITIS.

JOKE 28

Q: A GROUP OF DENTISTS DISCOVERED A NEW CHEMICAL ELEMENT. WHAT DID THEY NAME IT?

A: FLOSSPHORUS.

JOKE 29

Q: WHAT DOES THE DENTIST OF THE YEAR RECEIVE?

A: A LITTLE PLAQUE.

JOKE 30

Q: HOW DO TEETH FIND MATES AT A CARNIVAL?

A: AT THE KISSING TOOTH.

JOKE 31

Q: WHAT COMES OUT AT NIGHT AND GOES, "MUNCH, MUNCH, OUCH!"

A: A VAMPIRE WITH A ROTTEN TOOTH.

JOKE 32

Q: WHY ARE TEETH SO SHARP?

A: THEY STUDY A LOT!

JOKE 33

PATIENT: DOCTOR, I HAVE YELLOW TEETH, WHAT DO I DO?

DENTIST: WEAR A BROWN TIE.

JOKE 34

Q: WHAT DID THE DENTAL HYGIENIST HAVE TO CLEAN OUT FROM BETWEEN THE POLAR BEARS TEETH?

A: SLOW ESKIMOS.

JOKE 35

Q: WHAT DID THEY CALL THE TOOTH WHO WENT TO HARVARD?

A: THE WISDOM TOOTH.

JOKE 36

Q: WHY DID THE TREE GO TO THE DENTIST?

A: IT NEEDED A ROOT CANAL.

JOKE 37

Q: WHY IS 4,840 SQUARE YARDS LIKE A BAD TOOTH?

A: BECAUSE IT IS AN ACRE.

JOKE 38

Q: WHAT HAS TEETH BUT NO BITE?

A: A COMB.

JOKE 39

Q: WHAT IS RED, AND BAD FOR YOUR TEETH?

A: BRICK.

JOKE 40

Q: WHAT DO YOU CALL THE SOFT TISSUE BETWEEN A SHARK'S TEETH?

A: A SLOW SWIMMER.

JOKE 41

DENTIST: DON'T WORRY. I'M PAINLESS.

PATIENT: I'M NOT.

JOKE 42

Q: WHAT DID THE DENTIST SAY TO THE COMPUTER SCIENTIST?

A: THIS WON'T HURT A BYTE.

JOKE 43

Q: WHAT KIND OF FRUIT LEAVES CASH FOR TEETH THEY FIND?

A: THE TOOTH PEAR-IE.

JOKE 44

Q: WHAT DO YOU CALL A DENTIST WHO PULLED THE WRONG TOOTH?

A: AN ACCIDENTIST.

JOKE 45

Q: WHY DID THE ANTHROPOD NEED BRACES?

A: IT HAD A TRILOBITE.

JOKE 46

Q: WHAT IS THE TOOTH FAIRY'S FAVORITE CHRISTMAS SONG?

A: ALL I WANT FOR CHRISTMAS IS YOUR TWO FRONT TEETH!

JOKE 47

Q: WHAT IS A TOOTHACHE?

A: A PAIN THAT DRIVES PEOPLE TO EXTRACTION.

JOKE 48

Q: WHAT HAPPENED TO THE MAN WHO PUT HIS FALSE TEETH IN BACKWARDS?

A: HE ATE HIMSELF!

JOKE 49

Q: WHAT DID THE DENTAL HYGIENIST SEE AT THE NORTH POLE?

A: A MOLAR BEAR.

JOKE 50

Q: WHAT DID THE DENTIST WHISPER TO THE TOOTH AS SHE LEFT THE ROOM?

A: "I'LL FILL YOU IN WHEN I RETURN."

JOKE 51

DENTIST: YOUR TEETH ARE LIKE STARS.

PATIENT: BECAUSE THEY SHINE?

DENTIST: NO...SO YELLOW AND SO FAR APART.

JOKE 52

Q: HOW DOES SNOOP DOGG KEEP HIS TEETH WHITE?

A: BLEEEEEE-YATCH!

JOKE 53

Q: WHY DO REDHEADS HAVE BAD BREATH?

A: GINGER-VITIS.

JOKE 54

PATIENT: DOCTOR, I AM VERY NERVOUS. YOU KNOW, THIS IS MY FIRST EXTRACTION.

YOUNG DENTIST: DON'T WORRY, IT'S MY FIRST EXTRACTION TOO.

JOKE 55

Q: WHERE DO DENTISTS LIKE TO RETIRE?

A: FLUORIDA.

JOKE 56

Q: HOW DOES FOOD GET INTO A MOUTH?

A: BY PAYING AT THE TOLL TOOTH.

JOKE 57

Q: WHEN DO PEOPLE LOOK FORWARD TO FARTS?

A: WHEN THEIR FRIENDS HAVE HALITOSIS.

JOKE 58

Q: WHAT DID THE 95-YEAR-OLD SAY TO HER GREAT-GRANDSON?

A: I MISS THE DAYS OF BEING YOUR AGE WHEN MY TEETH WERE IN MY MOUTH 24/7!

JOKE 59

Q: WHICH CANDY LOST ALL ITS TEETH?

A: GUMMY BEARS.

JOKE 60

Q: WHO IS THE AUTHOR OF THE TOOTHY BEST SELLER, DENTAL EXAMINATION?

A: HOPE N. WIDE.

JOKE 61

Q: WHY DID THE DEER NEED BRACES?

A: HE HAD BUCK TEETH.

JOKE 62

Q: HOW CAN YOU GET A MAGNIFICENT SET OF TEETH PUT IN FOR FREE?

A: IRRITATE A SHARK.

JOKE 63

Q: WHAT DO YOU CALL A DENTIST IN ENGLAND?

A: UNEMPLOYED.

JOKE 64

Q: WHY DID THE TOOTH ASK FOR ALONE TIME?

A: IT NEEDED TIME TOOTHINK.

JOKE 65

Q: WHY DIDN'T THE PATIENT SHOW UP FOR THEIR ROOT CANAL?

A: THEY LOST THEIR NERVE.

JOKE 66

Q: WHAT DID THE MOUSE SAY WHEN HER FRIEND CHIPPED HER FRONT TEETH?

A: HARD CHEESE.

JOKE 67

Q: WHY DID THE DENTIST GO TO THE TOOTH SHOP?

A: TO BICUSPIDS.

JOKE 68

Q: WHAT KIND OF BREATH MINTS DO CANNIBALS EAT?

A: MEN-TOES.

JOKE 69

Q: WHY DID THE CHEERLEADER SCHEDULE A DENTIST APPOINTMENT?

A: SHE NEEDED A ROOT CANAL.

JOKE 70

Q: WHAT'S THE BEST THING TO PUT INTO A SLICE OF PUMPKIN PIE?

A: YOUR TEETH.

JOKE 71

Q: WHAT DO YOU CALL A DENTIST'S ADVICE?

A: HIS FL-OSSOPHY.

JOKE 72

Q: WHAT DO YOU CALL IT WHEN SOME PEOPLE HAVE 32 TEETH AND SOME HAVE 6?

A: SIMPLE METH.

JOKE 73

Q: WHY HAS A DENTIST'S JOB GOTTEN SO MUCH EASIER?

A: BECAUSE ALL THE KIDS ARE FLOSSING ALL THE TIME NOW.

JOKE 74

Q: WHY DID THE TOOTH FAIRY SEE A THERAPIST?

A: SHE NO LONGER BELIEVED IN HERSELF.

JOKE 75

Q: WHY ARE TEETH SO HARD?

A: THEY EXERCISE A LOT!

JOKE 76

Q: WHY DIDN'T THE DENTIST MARRY THE PATIENT HE LOVED?

A: HE COULDN'T AFFORD TO; SHE IS HIS BEST PATIENT.

JOKE 77

Q: HOW IS GOING TO THE DENTIST LIKE THOSE FILMS WHERE A CHARACTER GETS INTERROGATED?

A: IT'S OBVIOUS WHEN YOU'RE LYING – AND IF YOU DON'T COME CLEAN, YOU MIGHT LOSE A TOOTH.

JOKE 78

Q: WHAT DID THE JUDGE SAY TO THE DENTIST?

A: "DO YOU SWEAR TO PULL THE TOOTH, THE WHOLE TOOTH AND NOTHING BUT THE TOOTH?"

JOKE 79

Q: WHAT DO YOU CALL GEORGE WASHINGTON'S WOODEN TEETH?

A: PRESIDENTURES.

JOKE 80

Q: WHAT'S A DENTIST'S FAVORITE EMOTE TO USE WHEN THEY PLAY FORTNITE?

A: THE FLOSS.

JOKE 81

Q: HOW DO THE DENTIST AND THE MANICURIST FIGHT?

A: TOOTH AND NAIL.

JOKE 82

DENTIST: WHAT SORT OF AN ACT DO YOU DO?

PATIENT: I BEND OVER BACKWARDS AND PICK UP A SCARF WITH MY TEETH.

DENTIST: ANYTHING ELSE?

PATIENT: THEN I BEND OVER BACKWARDS AND PICK UP MY TEETH.

JOKE 83

Q: WHAT DO YOU CALL A DENTIST THAT DOESN'T LIKE TEA?

A: DENIS.

JOKE 84

Q: WHAT DID THE CANINE SAY TO THE MOLAR?

A: "THAR'S GOLD IN THEM THAR FILLS."

JOKE 85

Q: WHAT'S THE DIFFERENCE BETWEEN A THUNDERSTORM AND A LION WITH A TOOTHACHE?

A: ONE POURS WITH RAIN AND THE OTHER ROARS WITH PAIN.

JOKE 86

Q: WHAT DOES A TUBA PLAYER USE TO BRUSH HIS TEETH?

A: A TUBA TOOTHPASTE!

JOKE 87

Q: WHERE DO KILLER WHALES GO TO GET THEIR TEETH ALIGNED?

A: THE ORCADONTIST.

JOKE 88

Q: WHY DIDN'T THE MONSTER USE TOOTHPASTE?

A: BECAUSE HE SAID HIS TEETH WEREN'T LOOSE.

JOKE 89

Q: WHAT SONG DO DENTISTS LIKE TO SING?

A: THE YANKS ARE COMING.

JOKE 90

Q: WHY WAS THE PATIENT SO OFFENDED WHEN HER DENTIST SAID SHE HAD BAD BREATH?

A: SHE WAS TALKING TO SOMEONE IN THE WAITING ROOM AT THE TIME.

JOKE 91

Q: WHAT DOES A DENTIST CALL HIS X-RAYS?

A: TOOTH PICS.

JOKE 92

Q: WHAT IS A DRILL TEAM?

A: A GROUP OF DENTISTS WHO WORK TOGETHER.

JOKE 93

Q: "HAVE YOU EVER COME ACROSS A MAN WHO, AT THE SLIGHTEST TOUCH, CAUSED YOU TO THRILL AND TREMBLE IN EVERY FIBER OF YOUR BEING?"

A: "YES, THE DENTIST."

JOKE 94

Q: WHY DID THE GIRL BRING SPELUNKING GEAR TO HER DENTIST APPOINTMENT?

A: SHE HEARD SHE WAS THERE FOR A BIG CAVITY AND WANTED TO EXPLORE.

JOKE 95

Q: WHAT DID THE SEDATED PATIENT SAY TO THE DENTIST?

A: IF YOU STRIKE OIL, WE SHARE THE PROFITS.

JOKE 96

Q: WHAT DO YOU GET WHEN 20 METH HEADS GATHER IN A ROOM?

A: A FULL SET OF TEETH.

JOKE 97

Q: WHY DIDN'T THE DENTIST ASK HIS RECEPTIONIST OUT?

A: HE WAS ALREADY TAKING A TOOTH OUT.

JOKE 98

Q: WHY DO DENTISTS LIKE PASTA?

A: BECAUSE IT IS SO FILLING.

JOKE 99

Q: WHAT HAPPENS WHEN YOU GET A GOLD TOOTH?

A: YOU PUT YOUR MONEY WHERE YOUR MOUTH IS.

JOKE 100

Q: HOW DID THE DENTIST BECOME A BRAIN SURGEON?

A: THE DRILL SLIPPED.

JOKE 101

Q: WHY DID THE QUEEN GO TO THE DENTIST?

A: TO GET HER TEETH CROWNED.

JOKE 102

Q: WHAT DO YOU CALL AN ELDERLY DENTIST?

A: A BIT LONG IN THE TOOTH.

JOKE 103

Q: WHAT GAME ARE YOU PLAYING IF YOU DON'T BRUSH YOUR TEETH?

A: TOOTH OR DARE.

JOKE 104

Q: WHAT DO YOU CALL A DENTIST WHO CAN'T STOP PULLING TEETH?

A: ABSCESSIVE COMPULSIVE.

JOKE 105

Q. WHO WROTE THE BITING BOOK, I HAVE A TOOTHACHE?

A. PHIL A. CAVITY.

JOKE 106

Q: WHY DO DENTISTS SEEM MOODY?

A: BECAUSE THEY ALWAYS LOOK DOWN IN THE MOUTH.

JOKE 107

PATIENT TO DENTIST: "HOW MUCH TO STRAIGHTEN MY TEETH?"

DENTIST: "TEN THOUSAND BUCKS."

PATIENT HEADS FOR THE DOOR.

DENTIST TO PATIENT: "WHERE ARE YOU GOING?"

PATIENT: "TO A PLASTIC SURGEON TO GET MY MOUTH BENT."

JOKE 108

Q: WHY DID THE TERMITE EAT THE COUCH, THE CHAIR, AND THE COFFEE TABLE?

A: IT HAD A SUITE TOOTH.

JOKE 109

Q: WHAT DO YOU CALL TWO DENTISTS WHO LIVE ACROSS THE WORLD FROM EACH OTHER?

A: MOLAR OPPOSITES.

JOKE 110

Q: WHY WAS THE ORTHODONTIST INVESTIGATED BY THE SECURITIES & EXCHANGE COMMISSION?

A: FOR INCISOR TRADING.

JOKE 111

Q: WHAT FOUR WORDS DO DENTISTS WISH THEY COULD SOMETIMES SAY?

A: "I HATE YOU, TOO."

JOKE 112

Q: WHAT IS AN ORTHODONTIST'S FAVORITE DAY OF THE WEEK?

A: TOOTHSDAY.

JOKE 113

Q: WHAT DID THE DENTIST SAY TO TIGER WOODS?

A: "YOU HAVE A HOLE IN ONE. "

JOKE 114

Q: WHY DID THE DENTIST MARRY THE ORTHODONTIST?

A: THEY WERE SO ENAMELED OF EACH OTHER.

JOKE 115

Q: WHAT HAPPENED AFTER THE MAN WENT ON A DATE WITH A DENTAL HYGIENIST?

A: SHE SAID SHE HAD A GREAT TIME AND WOULD LIKE TO SEE HIM AGAIN IN 6 MONTHS...

JOKE 116

SON: WHY DO DENTISTS CALL THEIR OFFICES DENTAL PARLORS?

FATHER: BECAUSE THEY ARE DRAWING ROOMS, MY SON.

JOKE 117

DENTIST: JUST LET ME FINISH AND YOU WILL BE ANOTHER MAN AFTER THESE COSMETIC PROCEDURES.

PATIENT: OKAY DOC, BUT DON'T FORGET TO SEND YOUR BILL TO THE OTHER MAN.

JOKE 118

Q: WHY DID THE GURU REFUSE NOVOCAIN AT THE DENTIST?

A: HE WANTED TO TRANSCEND DENTAL MEDICATION.

JOKE 119

Q: WHAT DOES A DENTIST GIVE A HIPPO WITH A TOOTHACHE?

A: ANYTHING IT WANTS.

JOKE 120

Q: WHAT'S WORSE THAN HAVING YOUR DOCTOR TELL YOU THAT YOU HAVE VD?

A: HAVING YOUR DENTIST TELL YOU.

JOKE 121

Q: WHY ARE DENTISTS SO GOOD AT PROBLEM SOLVING?

A: THEY KNOW HOW TO GET TO THE ROOT OF A PROBLEM.

JOKE 122

Q: WHY DID THE LUMBERJACK VISIT THE DENTIST?

A: HE HAD A CAVITREE.

JOKE 123

Q: DID YOU KNOW I'M DATING A DENTAL HYGIENIST?

A: SHE HAS THE CLEANEST TEETH I'VE EVER COME ACROSS.

JOKE 124

Q: WHAT WILL THE DENTIST GIVE YOU FOR $1?

A: BUCK TEETH!

JOKE 125

Q: WHY DID JILL TELL GUS HE HAS COLDPLAY TEETH?

A: BECAUSE THEY'RE ALL YELLOW.

JOKE 126

Q: HOW LONG DID IT TAKE FOR THE TWO TEETH TO FALL FOR EACH OTHER?

A: IT WAS LOVE AT FIRST BITE!

JOKE 127

Q: WHICH EGYPTIAN HAD THE HEALTHIEST TEETH?

A: KING TOOTHANKHAMUN.

JOKE 128

Q: WHAT HAS 132 LEGS AND 8 TEETH?

A: THE FRONT ROW OF A TOBY KEITH CONCERT.

JOKE 129

Q: HOW IS A TOOTHLESS DOG LIKE A TREE?

A: IT HAS MORE BARK THAN BITE.

JOKE 130

Q: WHY DID THE SNOWMAN GO TO THE ORTHODONTIST?

A: TO CORRECT HIS FROST BITE.

Q. WHAT'S THE BEST WAY TO FIND A PAINLESS DENTIST IN YOUR NEIGHBORHOOD?

A. WORD OF MOUTH.

Q: WHAT DO YOU GET WHEN YOU CROSS A CACTUS WITH A GIRAFFE?

A: A LONG NECKED TOOTHBRUSH.

JOKE 133

Q: IF YOU BRUSH YOUR TEETH AT NIGHT TO KEEP YOUR TEETH, WHY DO YOU BRUSH YOUR TEETH IN THE MORNING?

A: TO KEEP YOUR FRIENDS.

JOKE 134

Q: WHAT GAME DID THE DENTAL STUDENTS PLAY?

A: CAPS AND ROBBERS.

JOKE 135

Q: WHY COULDN'T THE TOOTH STAY FOR DINNER?

A: HE WAS IN A BRUSH.

JOKE 136

Q: WHY DON'T DENTISTS LIKE PHD HOLDERS?

A: BECAUSE PEOPLE CALL THEM DOCTORS.

JOKE 137

Q: IF BELLA HAS 20 SODAS AND DRINKS 15 OF THEM, WHAT DOES SHE HAVE?

A: CAVITIES!

JOKE 138

Q: WHAT ARE THE SIX MOST FRIGHTENING WORDS IN THE WORLD?

A: "THE DENTIST WILL SEE YOU NOW."

JOKE 139

Q: WHY DID THE PHARAOH VISIT THE DENTIST?

A: BECAUSE EGYPT HIS TOOTH....

JOKE 140

Q: WHY DIDN'T THE YELLOW TOOTH LAUGH AT THE WHITE TOOTH'S JOKES?

A: BECAUSE IT WAS ALREADY DEAD INSIDE.

JOKE 141

PATIENT: TELL ME HONESTLY, HOW AM I?

DENTIST: YOUR TEETH ARE FINE, BUT YOUR GUMS WILL HAVE TO COME OUT.

JOKE 142

Q: WHAT DID THE DENTIST TELL THE PARSIMONIOUS PATIENT?

A: "NO, WE DON'T GIVE DISCOUNTS FOR EMPTY SPACES WHEN CLEANING TEETH, MRS. BARB!"

JOKE 143

A MAN AND A WOMAN ARE RIDING ON A BUS.

WOMAN: EVERY TIME YOU SMILE, I FEEL LIKE INVITING YOU TO MY PLACE.

MAN: NICE! ARE YOU SINGLE?

WOMAN: NO. I'M A DENTIST.

JOKE 144

PATIENT: IF I GIVE UP SODA, CANDY AND POPCORN, WILL MY BRACES COME OFF SOONER?

DENTIST: NOT REALLY. IT WILL JUST SEEM LONGER.

JOKE 145

PATIENT: DO YOU EXTRACT TEETH PAINLESSLY?

DENTIST: NOT ALWAYS, THE OTHER DAY I NEARLY DISLOCATED MY WRIST.

JOKE 146

Q: WHY DID THE GIRL WANT A BONE?

A: THE DENTIST SAID HER CANINES WERE COMING IN.

JOKE 147

Q: WHERE DOES MOST OF A HOCKEY PLAYER'S SALARY COME FROM?

A: THE TOOTH FAIRY.

JOKE 148

Q: HOW DO YOU KNOW IF YOU HAVE BAD BREATH?

A: WHEN YOU SHOUT AT YOUR DOG AND HE TRIES CHEWING IT.

JOKE 149

Q: WHAT DO YOU CALL IT WHEN DENTISTS HAVE A TV ON THE CEILING SO PATIENTS CAN WATCH SHOWS WHILE THEY WORK?

A: NETFLIX AND DRILL.

JOKE 150

Q: WHAT DID THE PHILOSOPHICAL DENTIST ASK HIMSELF?

A: "TOTHEE OR NOT TOOTHEE, THAT IS THE QUESTION."

JOKE 151

Q: WHICH TEETH DO YOU HAVE TO BRUSH?

A: THE ONES YOU WANT TO KEEP!

JOKE 152

Q: WHAT TYPE OF SODA DO DENTISTS LIKE?

A: ALL OF THEM.

JOKE 153

Q: WHICH UNKNOWN COMIC DENTIST WROTE THE BOOK, PAIN MANAGEMENT?

A: NOVA CAINE.

JOKE 154

Q: WHY DID THE ORTHODONTIST FAINT WHEN HER SON WALKED THROUGH THE DOOR?

A: HE TOLD HER HE SIGNED UP FOR THE HOCKEY TEAM.

JOKE 155

Q: WHY DID THE SMARTPHONE NEED TOOTH WHITENING?

A: IT HAD A LITTLE BLUETOOTH THAT NEED TO BE TAKEN CARE OF.

JOKE 156

Q: HOW MANY DENTISTS DOES IT TAKE TO CHANGE A LIGHTBULB?

A: ONE TO ADMINISTER THE ANESTHETIC, ONE TO EXTRACT THE LIGHTBULB, AND ONE TO OFFER THE SOCKET MOUTHWASH.

JOKE 157

Q: WHY SHOULD YOU BE NICE TO YOUR DENTIST?

A: BECAUSE THEY HAVE FILLINGS TOO.

JOKE 158

Q: WHAT DO YOU NAME A TOOTH THAT YOU LOSE IN YOUR YARD?

A: A LAWN MOLAR.

JOKE 159

Q: HAS YOUR TOOTH STOPPED HURTING YET?

A: I DON'T KNOW, THE DENTIST KEPT IT.

JOKE 160

Q: WHY DID THE DOUGHNUT GO TO THE DENTIST?

A: FOR A FILLING!

JOKE 161

Q: WHAT IS THE DIFFERENCE BETWEEN A DENTIST AND A PERSONAL TRAINER?

A: THE DENTIST LETS YOU SIT DOWN WHILE SHE HURTS YOU.

JOKE 162

Q: WHAT TIME OF DAY DO DENTISTS LIKE TO SCHEDULE APPOINTMENTS?

A: TOOTH-HURTY (2:30).

JOKE 163

Q: WHAT IS A DENTIST'S FAVORITE MOVIE?

A: PLAQUE TO THE FUTURE!

JOKE 164

Q: WHY DOES DONKEY KONG FLOSS?

A: TO PREVENT TOOTH DK.

JOKE 165

Q: WHAT'S THE DIFFERENCE BETWEEN A GOOD DENTIST AND A GREAT DENTIST?

A: A GOOD DENTIST IS A LITTLE PICKY, A GREAT DENTIST NEVER GETS ON YOUR NERVES.

JOKE 166

Q: WHAT DID THE MAN SUFFERING FROM BAD BREATH DO?

A: HE SENT HIS WIFE TO THE DENTIST.

JOKE 167

Q: WHAT DID THE POKÉMON MASTER SAY TO HIS TOOTH WHEN HE PULLED IT OUT?

A: "I CHEWS YOU!"

JOKE 168

Q: WHY DID THE BLONDE GO TO THE DENTIST?

A: SOMEONE DENTED HER CAR.

JOKE 169

Q: WHY DIDN'T THE DENTIST LET JACK NICHOLSON KEEP HIS EXTRACTED WISDOM TEETH?

A: HE CAN'T HANDLE THE TOOTH!

JOKE 170

Q: HOW FAR IS IT TO THE ORTHODONTIST'S OFFICE?

A: SIXSMILES.

JOKE 171

Q: WHAT DID THE TOOTH SAY DURING THE DENTIST APPOINTMENT?

A: "FILL 'ER UP!"

JOKE 172

Q: WHAT IS AN ORTHODONTIST'S FAVORITE PLACE TO SHOP?

A: THE GAP.

JOKE 173

Q: WHAT TYPE OF FILLING DO YOU WANT IN YOUR TOOTH?

A: CHOCOLATE!

JOKE 174

Q: WHAT'S THE DIFFERENCE BETWEEN AMERICAN AND BRITISH DENTISTS?

A: BRITISH DENTISTS TEND TO BE GENTLER WITH THEIR PATIENTS WHEREAS AMERICAN DENTISTS TEND TO YANK TEETH.

JOKE 175

Q: WHAT DID THE DENTIST IN THE PORNO SAY?

A: "YOUR TEETH ARE THE WHITEST I'VE COME ACROSS."

JOKE 176

Q: WHY DID THE GOD OF THUNDER LOSE HIS VOICE AFTER HIS WISDOM TEETH EXTRACTION?

A: BECAUSE HE WAS TOO THOR.

Q: WHAT DID THE VAMPIRE CALL HIS FALSE TEETH?

A: A NEW FANGLED DEVICE.

Q: WHAT DID ONE TOOTH SAY TO THE OTHER?

A: GET YOUR CAP ON, THE DENTIST IS TAKING US OUT TONIGHT.

JOKE 179

Q: WHY DID THE DENTIST LEAVE THE AIRPORT?

A: HE WAS AFRAID OF THE CAVITY SEARCH.

JOKE 180

Q: WHAT ARE DENTISTS INCAPABLE OF?

A: ASKING QUESTIONS THAT REQUIRE A SIMPLE YES OR NO ANSWER.

JOKE 181

Q: WHAT DO YOU GET WHEN YOU CROSS TEETH WITH CANDY?

A: DENTAL FLOSS.

JOKE 182

Q: DENTIST: WHEN DID YOU LAST FLOSS?

A: PATIENT: YOU SHOULD KNOW, YOU WERE THERE.

JOKE 183

Q: WHY CAN'T TEETH WORK AT THE ORANGE JUICE FACTORY?

A: BECAUSE THEY WILL EAT ALL THE PULP.

JOKE 184

Q: HOW ARE DENTURES LIKE STARS?

A: THEY COME OUT AT NIGHT.

JOKE 185

DENTIST: YOU HAVE NICE, EVEN TEETH.

PATIENT: REALLY?

DENTIST: UNFORTUNATELY, IT'S BECAUSE TEETH NOS. 1, 3 AND 5 ARE MISSING.

JOKE 186

MOTHER: DON'T YOU FEEL BETTER NOW THAT YOU'VE GONE TO THE DENTIST?

DAUGHTER: SURE DO... HE WASN'T IN.

JOKE 187

Q: WHICH TEETH ARE THE BRIGHTEST?

A: THE WISDOM TEETH.

JOKE 188

Q: WHAT HAPPENED WHEN A MAN FELL IN LOVE WITH A GRAND PIANO?

A: HE SAID, "DARLING, YOU'VE GOT LOVELY TEETH."

Q: WHAT DO MOLAR BEARS FIGHT FOR?

A: THEY FIGHT AGAINST ENAMEL CRUELTY.

Q: WHAT DID THE DENTIST SAY WHEN HE EXTRACTED A TOOTH?

A: "I'M SORRY FOR YOUR FLOSS."

JOKE 191

Q: WHY IS THE TOOTH FAIRY SO SMART?

A: SHE HAS A LOT OF WISDOM TEETH.

JOKE 192

Q: WHY DID ANIMAL CONTROL CALL THE DENTIST?

A: THEIR CANINES WERE LOOSE.

JOKE 193

Q: HOW DO YOU KNOW THE TOOTH FAIRY IS A JOURNALIST?

A: THEY'RE ALWAYS SEARCHING FOR THE TOOTH.

JOKE 194

Q: WHY DO YOU FORGET A TOOTH, AS SOON AS THE DENTIST PULLS IT OUT?

A: BECAUSE IT GOES RIGHT OUT OF YOUR HEAD.

JOKE 195

Q: WHAT'S A DENTIST'S FAVORITE DINOSAUR?

A: A FLOSSIRAPTOR.

JOKE 196

Q: HOW DID THE DENTIST FIND HIS NEW RECEPTIONIST?

A: BY WORD OF MOUTH.

JOKE 197

DENTIST: I NEED YOUR HELP. COULD YOU GIVE OUT A FEW OF YOUR LOUDEST, MOST PAINFUL SCREAMS?

PATIENT: WHY? DOC, IT ISN'T ALL THAT BAD THIS TIME.

DENTIST: THERE ARE SO MANY PEOPLE IN THE WAITING ROOM RIGHT NOW, AND I DON'T WANT TO MISS THE 4 O'CLOCK GAME.

JOKE 198

Q: WHAT'S BROWN AND VERY BAD FOR YOUR DENTAL HEALTH?

A: A BASEBALL BAT.

JOKE 199

Q: WHAT DOES A DENTIST CALL AN ASTRONAUT'S CAVITY?

A: A BLACK HOLE.

JOKE 200

Q: WHAT DO YOU CALL A BOAT FULL OF DENTAL WORKERS?

A: A TOOTH FERRY.

Printed in Great Britain
by Amazon

54791098R00059